The KidHaven Science Library

Biomes

by Renee Kirchner

KIDHAVEN PRESS
An imprint of Thomson Gale, a part of The Thomson Corporation

THOMSON
TM
GALE

Detroit • New York • San Francisco • San Diego • New Haven, Conn. • Waterville, Maine • London • Munich

© 2006 Thomson Gale, a part of The Thomson Corporation.

Thomson and Star Logo are trademarks and Gale and KidHaven Press are registered trademarks used herein under license.

For more information, contact
KidHaven Press
27500 Drake Rd.
Farmington Hills, MI 48331-3535
Or you can visit our Internet site at http://www.gale.com

LIBRARY OF CONGRESS CATALOGING-IN-PUBLICATION DATA

Kirchner, Renee, 1964–
    Biomes / by Renee Kirchner.
        p. cm. — (The KidHaven science library)
    Includes bibliographical references.
    ISBN 0-7377-3052-8 (hard cover : alk. paper) 1. Biotic communities—Juvenile literature. I. Title. II. Series.
    QH541.14.K57 2006
    577—dc22
                                                                      2005017636

Printed in the United States of America

Contents

Chapter 1

Tundra

Tall grasses sway in the warm breeze. Many miles away, monkeys howl in the lush forest. Far to the north, a snowy owl spies its prey on the frozen ground. Near the equator, a snake seeks shelter from the heat. Dolphins dive and play in the ocean waters. Each of these scenes describes a different biome. A biome is a major community of plants and animals that lives in a certain type of **climate.**

Scientists disagree on the number of biomes, but biomes are generally grouped into five main categories: tundra, grasslands, deserts, forests, and aquatic. Every place on Earth is in one biome or another. An area is classified as a particular biome depending upon its climate, its type of soil, and the plants and animals that live there.

A Cold Climate

The tundra biome is in the Arctic Circle and covers nearly one-fifth of the land on Earth. It includes Alaska, northern Canada, and northern Asia. North of the tundra lies the Arctic Ocean, and pine tree forests are to the south.

The tundra is sometimes classified as desert because less than 10 inches (25.4cm) of **precipitation** fall on it a year. Most of this precipitation is snow. Snow can fall in the tundra in any season of the year, even in summer.

Because of its extreme northern location, the tundra receives sunlight both day and night in the summer months. In winter the tundra gets no sunshine at all for many weeks. Summers are very short, with cool temperatures that never rise above 59°F (15°C). Winter temperatures can fall as low as −50°F (−46°C).

The polar bear is a year-round resident of the tundra.

Treeless Land

The lack of moisture, light, and warmth in the tundra means that this biome has fewer kinds of plants than any other biome. Most of these plants have shallow roots or no roots at all. This is because the cold temperatures keep the ground frozen most of the year. Only the top layer thaws during the summer growing season. At that time the roots of growing plants spread out horizontally, because they cannot dig down into the frozen soil beneath. Plants whose roots grow deep, such as most trees, cannot survive in the tundra. In fact the word *tundra* is from a Finnish word that means "treeless land."

Because the ground of the tundra is frozen for much of the year, the growing season lasts only two to three months. For this reason, most tundra plants are very small. As soon as the snow melts in June, plants begin to grow as fast as possible. Wildflowers such as arctic lupine and purple milk vetch grow very quickly and are some of the first plants to be seen each summer. These flowers cover the tundra in a blanket of color.

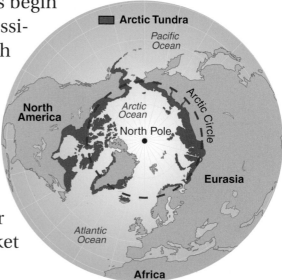

Caribou migrate to the tundra in the spring when new plants emerge.

Plants in the tundra have developed **adaptations** to survive the cold, windy climate. One example of a hardy tundra plant is the cushion plant, which looks like a round chair cushion. This plant hugs the ground and has densely packed leaves to shield the branches from snow, wind, and ice. These adaptations allow the center of the cushion plant to maintain a constant temperature when the air is windy and cold.

Yellow arctic poppies thrive in the tundra through a different adaptation. They have tiny hairs all over their leaves and stems. The hairs trap water to keep the plants from drying out.

Lichens are perfectly adapted to the tundra because they do not need soil or rain to survive. They absorb moisture from water vapor and minerals from airborne dust. Lichens are made up of algae and fungi and look like colorful splashes of paint. These hardy plants grow on rocks and fence posts.

Tundra Visitors

Tundra grasses, flowering plants, and lichen are plentiful only during the summer, so this is when many animals and birds **migrate** to the tundra to feed, hunt, and breed. The animal population here constantly changes. More animals live in the tundra in the summer than in the winter. Summer visitors include lynx, brown bears, coyotes, and a wide

Musk oxen have two coats of fur to protect them from tundra winters.

variety of birds. Birds come by the millions to lay eggs and raise chicks.

Each spring thousands of caribou migrate to the tundra from forests to the south. Caribou are large deer. Their migration is timed so the animals arrive in the tundra just as new plants emerge. Calves are born soon afterward. The herd grows healthy and fat off the nutritious grasses and plants before migrating back south for the winter.

Surviving the Cold

A few animals and birds that have developed adaptations to survive the cold, harsh winter conditions live on the tundra year-round. Warm coats protect some of these animals from the cold. For example, musk oxen, which resemble buffalo, have two furry coats that keep heat from escaping their bodies. One layer is a woolly undercoat called a qiviut, and the other is a long, hairy overcoat.

Other animals simply take shelter from the cold. Lemmings are small mammals that look like rodents. They burrow under the snow. The snow insulates their home, keeps them warm, and hides them from **predators.**

The tundra has less plant and animal diversity than most other biomes. The plants and animals of the tundra are uniquely suited to survive its harsh, cold environment and short growing season.

Chapter 2

Grasslands

The grassland biome is well named, because it is covered with various types of grasses. Grasslands are found on every continent except Antarctica. They can be classified as **temperate** or **tropical.** A temperate grassland has a climate that is neither too hot nor too cold. A grassland with a hot, wet climate is known as tropical.

Temperate grasslands are known by many names. In Europe and Asia, grasslands called steppes stretch almost a third of the way around the world. South America has pastures known as pampas. Australia's rangeland is one of the world's main farming regions, as are the prairies of North America. Finally, there is the veld of South Africa.

It is rain, more than any other factor, that influences whether an area is a grassland. Grasslands receive just enough rain to support grass, but not enough to support trees. Temperate grasslands receive 10 to 30 inches (25 to 76cm) of rain every year. The grassland rainy season is during late spring and early summer. **Droughts** often occur in late summer.

The tropical grassland biome, known as the savanna, covers about 5 million square miles (8 million sq. km) in central Africa. There are also savanna areas in Australia, South America, and India. Their average rainfall is 20 to 50 inches (50.8 to 127cm) per year. The savanna has a rainy season followed by a dry season, which prevents trees from growing.

The grass on the African savanna supports many animals, including zebras.

Many grasslands have been turned into farm-land. They have rich, dark soils that are better for growing crops than soils in other biomes. The crops grown on these lands feed billions of people. In fact so much food is produced on grasslands that they are sometimes called "Earth's breadbasket."

Grassland Plants

The word *grass* is used for approximately 9,000 different plants found in grasslands worldwide. Even though grasses may look very different, they have many things in common. First, grasses do not have woody tissue as trees or shrubs do. Second, all grasses are flowering plants. Their flowers are not showy or colorful like garden flowers, but rather

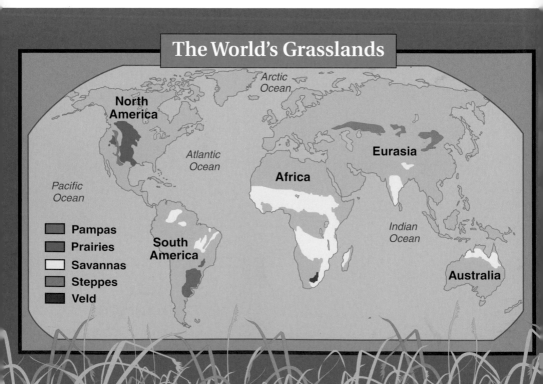

The World's Grasslands

The yellow seed heads of Indian grass are a common sight on the tallgrass prairie of North America.

they are very small and usually the same color as the grass itself. Finally, all grasses grow from the bottom up rather than from the top. This growth pattern helps them survive the herds of **grazing** animals that sometimes live in grasslands.

Indian grass is a preferred grass of grazing animals in the tallgrass prairie of North America. The seed heads of Indian grass are yellow with white hairs, and the plant has long, flat leaves called blades. Indian grass can reach a height of 8 feet (2.4m), which is taller than a professional basketball player. When grazing animals chew the grass, they sometimes crop it close to the ground. This would kill plants that grow from the tips of their twigs or branches. But grass plants survive because new shoots grow from the crown, which is located at the surface of the ground. Since the crown is so close to the ground, it is not damaged by grazing animals.

Plants in grasslands must be able to survive not only grazing animals, but extremely windy conditions as well. The land is flat, and there are no trees to break the wind. Grasses have thin, flat blades on tall, flexible stems. This is the perfect structure to survive strong winds. The stems bend with the wind rather than breaking off.

Like prairie grasses, plants that grow on a savanna must survive heat, drought, and wind. One plant that is well adapted to drought is elephant grass. Its roots reach below the ground to a depth equal to the grass's height. The plant can reach heights of up to 10 feet (3m) during rainy seasons. During dry seasons, the stems and leaves may die, but the deep roots remain in the soil. The grass grows back when it rains again.

Wide-Open Spaces

The wide-open spaces of the prairie offer few places for animals to hide from predators. To survive, prairie dogs have adapted by building their own hiding places. These small ground squirrels dig huge underground burrows where they live in groups called colonies. They emerge above ground only to eat. Prairie dogs take turns guarding their colony. When a predator appears, the guard makes a sharp barking sound that warns the other prairie dogs to flee back into the burrow.

A similar animal lives in the steppes of Europe and Asia. Steppe marmots also live in underground burrows. Unlike prairie dogs, they do not live in colonies. They prefer instead to live in their own dens.

Large mammals cannot burrow underground, so they live in herds for protection from predators. One example is the pronghorn antelope, which lives in western North America. In a herd of pronghorn, several animals act as lookouts. Pronghorn have keen eyesight that allows them to spot predators, such as coyotes, approaching from great distances. When a lookout spies a predator, it starts to

A herd of pronghorn antelope relies on lookouts to spot predators.

The cheetah is a fast-moving predator that hunts on the wide-open savanna.

run and other pronghorns follow. The animals can reach speeds of up to 60 miles (96km) per hour.

Some of the fastest and fiercest predators live and hunt their **prey** on the wide-open spaces of the savanna. The cheetah is a savanna predator built for speed. Its long, thin body and powerful back legs help it move quickly and gracefully. In addition, cheetahs have large nostrils and lungs that allow them to take in plenty of air. This means they can breathe easily while running. They hunt early in the morning and late in the afternoon by scanning the countryside and taking chase. Cheetahs can reach speeds up to 71 miles (114km) per hour, but their sprints rarely last more than a minute.

Grasslands are beautiful natural areas with wide-open spaces. They are home to many plants and animals that are well suited to this biome.

Chapter 3

Deserts

The desert biome covers 20 percent of Earth's land surface. Deserts can be found on six continents—Africa, Antarctica, Asia, Australia, South America, and North America. Many deserts, such as the Sahara, are found near the equator. Other deserts, such as the Gobi Desert in Asia, are located far north of the equator.

A desert is not just a hot place, as many people believe. Deserts may be hot or cold. All deserts are dry and have harsh conditions. A biome is classified as a desert if it receives 10 inches (25cm) or less of rain per year. Some deserts have not received any rain for years. A desert may be defined as arid, semiarid, or extremely arid. An arid desert is hot and dry year-round and changes little from season to season. A semiarid desert has more defined seasons, and the least amount of rain falls in the winter.

Water-Conserving Foliage

Plants that live in deserts must survive without a constant source of water. Some desert plants do

this by storing water in their leaves or stems. This makes the plant appear swollen like a water balloon. These types of plants are called succulents.

Succulents come in many different shapes and sizes. One type is the barrel cactus, which grows in the Sonoran, Mojave, and Chihuahuan deserts of the southwestern United States. The stem of the barrel cactus has folds like the pleats of an accordion. The folds keep the water-filled parts of the stem from drying out in the sun.

Another type of succulent is the lithop, or "living stone," which grows in South Africa. When its two leaves fill with water, this ground-hugging plant looks like a pair of stones. Its resemblance to a rock protects the lithop from plant-eating insects and rodents that eat plants.

Sun Protection

While some desert plants store water, others have long tap roots that reach water deep underground. One example of a plant with a long tap root is the mesquite tree, found in the Sonoran and Chihuahuan deserts. Although the trees are only the size of shrubs, their roots can grow up to 190 feet (57.9m) deep underground.

Desert plants also need protection from the drying effects of sunlight. Some plants, such as the aloe

The barrel cactus stores water to survive in the dry desert environment. Its sharp spines (inset) protect it from animals.

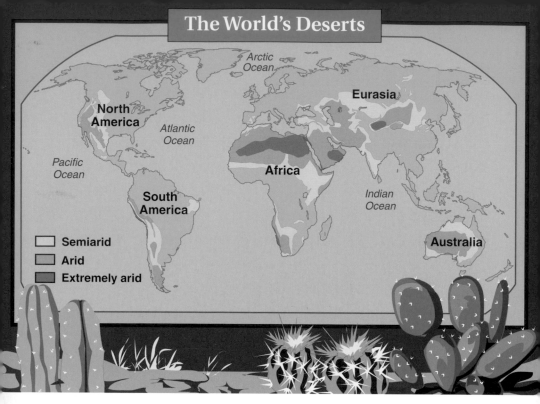

The World's Deserts

Semiarid
Arid
Extremely arid

plant, are protected from the sun's rays by a waxy coating on the stems and leaves. This coating acts like a sheet of plastic wrap around each leaf, holding water inside the plant.

Many plants have adapted to hot, dry desert conditions by reducing the size of their leaves or shedding their leaves altogether. This reduces the amount of water that is lost through **evaporation.** For example, the ocotillo plant of the southwestern United States remains leafless for part of the year, but it can grow leaves quickly after a rainfall. The tiny round leaves are shed again when water is scarce.

Another drought-tolerant plant is the creosote bush of North America. This bush has small green leaves and bright yellow flowers. The leaves of the creosote bush lose their color and shrivel when there is a severe drought. New buds grow underneath the old leaves. When rain falls, the old leaves are shed and new buds quickly replace them.

Adaptable Animals

Desert plants provide food and water to the many reptiles, insects, small mammals, and birds that live in the desert. Most desert animals are small, because deserts do not have the amount of food and water that large animals need to survive. It is also easier for small animals than for larger ones to find shelter under rocks or in burrows in the sand. Some large animals such as camels, oryx, and antelope do spend much of their lives in deserts. Other large animals, however, such as jackals and wild dogs, go into the desert only to hunt.

The Australian bandicoot is nocturnal. It sleeps during the hot day and hunts for food in the cool evening.

The fennec fox of the Sahara releases excess heat through its oversized ears.

Desert animals have special features or habits that allow them to survive in the hot, dry climate. Many animals are nocturnal, or active during the night, to avoid the hottest part of the day. Bandicoots are one example. These **marsupials** from Australia and New Guinea are about 11 to 32 inches (28 to 81cm) long and have long tails, large ears, and pointed snouts. They tunnel into burrows during the day and search for food such as fruit, seeds, and insects at night.

The fennec fox of the Sahara has a different way to stay cool. This animal rids itself of excess body heat through its oversized ears. Even though the fennec fox is the smallest fox, at only 8 to 10 inches (20.3 to 25.4cm) tall, it has huge ears. These ears allow excess heat to transfer from the animal into the outside air.

Conserving Water

Some animals, such as the kangaroo rat of California, do not need to drink water to survive. They get all the water they need from the seeds they eat. Many seeds are 20 to 50 percent water. In addition, kangaroo rats conserve the water they take in from the seeds. They produce urine that resembles a dry paste rather than a liquid.

Desert biomes are harsh environments of great natural beauty. Although they may appear barren and lifeless, deserts are home to many unique plants and animals.

Chapter 4

Forests

The forest biome covers about one-third of Earth's land area. Forests can be classified into three types: boreal, temperate, and tropical. Boreal (or taiga) forests cover parts of Canada, Alaska, Russia, and Scandinavia. Temperate forests are located in eastern North America, northeastern Asia, and Europe. Tropical rain forests are found near the equator.

More precipitation falls in the forest biome than in any other biome. They are classified into one type or another based upon the amount of precipitation they receive and their climate. Boreal forests receive 15 to 25 inches (28 to 63cm) per year, much of it as snow. Temperate forests, on the other hand, receive 30 to 60 inches (76.2 to 152.4cm) per year. Precipitation in the temperate forest is a mixture of snow and rain, depending on the season of the year. Tropical rain forests receive an amazing 150 inches (381cm) of rain per year.

Forest biomes are important to Earth because trees and plants give off oxygen, which humans and animals breathe. Trees also use up carbon dioxide, a gas that in high concentrations is poisonous to

Forest trees give off the oxygen that animals need to survive.

humans and animals. For these reasons, forests have been called the "lungs of the world."

A huge variety of plant and animal life lives in the forest biome. The rain forest alone has more than 1.5 million species of plants and animals. Only the aquatic biome has as many species as the forest biome.

Trees and More

Boreal forests consist of mostly cold-tolerant **conifers** such as pine, spruce, and fir trees. Conifer trees are ideally suited to the cold, snowy environment. They are covered with slippery needles rather than leaves. This lets snow slide off them rather than collect on the trees, which could break their branches. Conifers also have waterproof bark and branches that bend to allow additional snow to fall off. One example of a conifer tree is the ponderosa pine found in Canada and along the Pacific coast of the United States. It is a giant of a tree, growing from 100 to 160 feet (30.5 to 48.7m) tall. Its pine needles are dark green and grow in bundles of two or three. It is easy to recognize this pine tree by its orange-brown bark with deep ridges.

Temperate forests contain mainly **deciduous** trees. Deciduous trees are perfectly adapted to the changing seasons of the temperate forest. Their

Conifers such as this ponderosa pine have cones and needles (inset) rather than flowers and leaves.

broad green leaves capture sunlight in the summer to make food for the plant through a process called **photosynthesis.** Their leaves fall off in winter, and the places where the leaves were attached are sealed over. This protects the tree from freezing. One type of deciduous tree that is common in New England and Canada is the sugar maple tree. It can grow 100 feet (30.4m) tall. During the spring and summer, the 3- to 5-inch (7.6 to 12.7cm) leaves are dark green, and they turn a brilliant orange in the fall.

While boreal and temperate forests mainly consist of trees, the rain forest has a huge variety of plant life. The rain forest has three main layers of vegetation: the canopy, the understory, and the forest floor. The canopy is like a giant umbrella of tree branches. The understory is the dark, shady place

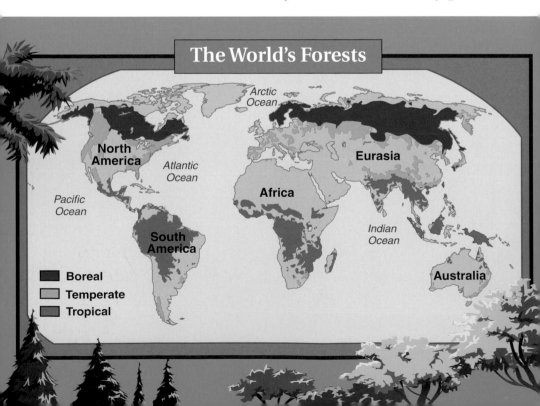

The World's Forests

Arctic Ocean

North America

Atlantic Ocean

Eurasia

Pacific Ocean

Africa

South America

Indian Ocean

Australia

■ Boreal
□ Temperate
■ Tropical

below the canopy. Smaller trees, bushes, and vines grow here. The forest floor is the basement of the rain forest. Leaves and plants rot on the forest floor.

The tropical rain forest is home to some of the most rare and unusual species of plants in the world. This biome can support a large variety of

The rare Rafflesia arnoldii flower can reach 3 feet in diameter.

plant life because it has lots of sunlight, rain, and warm temperatures year-round. One example of a tropical plant found only in the rain forest is the Rafflesia arnoldii, a rare, bright red flower that grows in Indonesia. It weighs 15 pounds (6.8kg) and measures 3 feet (0.9m) in diameter. That is as wide as a beanbag chair! In addition to its enormous size, the Rafflesia arnoldii is unusual in another way. Unlike other flowers that smell sweet, the Rafflesia arnoldii smells like rotting meat.

Forest Animals

Like plants, forest animals are uniquely suited to their surroundings. Animals that live in the boreal forest, for example, are well adapted for cold winters and a lot of snow. One such animal is the snowshoe hare, which has very large, furry hind feet that look like snowshoes. These big feet distribute the hare's weight evenly over a wide area of snow so that it does not sink. This allows the hare to travel quickly over deep snow to escape from predators such as coyotes, foxes, and great horned owls. Other mammals, such as ermine (short-tailed weasels), spend much of the winter under the snow. Ermine build dens in hollow logs or under tree roots. Sometimes they even take over the burrows of mice or ground squirrels.

While the animals of the boreal forests must adapt to cold and snow, animals of other forest environments face different challenges. Animals in the temperate forest often communicate with

The snowshoe hare often escapes from predators by using its long feet to run on top of deep snow.

An eastern gray squirrel keeps an eye out for danger.

sounds, because the thick growth of trees makes it hard for them to see each other. When the eastern gray squirrel is alarmed, for example, it alerts other squirrels with a distinctive barking noise. It also communicates with clucking and fussing sounds. Another noisy forest dweller is the tree toad. Male tree toads use a mating call in late spring and early summer to attract females. Some tree toads can be heard a mile away.

A common characteristic of almost all animals in the rain forest is their ability to live in trees. In fact some animals in the rain forest rarely ever climb down to the ground. The three-toed sloth is one of these animals. It cannot move quickly, so it would

The three-toed sloth is a tree-dwelling resident of the rain forest.

be an easy target for predators on the ground. In the trees, however, the sloth is **camouflaged** from predators such as large snakes and jaguars by its gray fur covered in blue-green algae. This coloring helps it blend in with both the tree trunks and leaves.

Forest biomes are very important to Earth because they are home to millions of plant and animal species. In addition, the trees in the forest provide plenty of life-giving oxygen to humans and animals.

Chapter 5

Aquatic

The aquatic biome is the world's largest biome. Fully 75 percent of Earth is covered with water. The aquatic biome can be broken down into two regions: freshwater and marine.

Freshwater is defined as water without salt. Freshwater biomes are made up of moving water, such as rivers and streams, and still water, such as lakes and ponds.

The marine biome is made up of bodies of water that contain salt, and it consists of oceans, coral reef habitats, and estuaries. There are five oceans: the Pacific, Atlantic, Indian, Arctic, and Southern (Antarctic). Coral reefs are huge underwater structures built by tiny animals called coral polyps. These structures are found in shallow, warm water and are home to many colorful animals. An estuary is a place where freshwater from rivers flows into salt water in the ocean.

Aquatic Plant Life

Plants that grow in rivers and streams have features to keep moving water from washing them away. For example, common water moss attaches itself to rocks or logs with rootlike structures called rhizoids. In addition, the plant's stem is very strong in the middle, like a rope. This lets it stand up to the movement of the water without breaking. Common water moss can be found in North America, Europe, Asia, and Africa. This dark green plant has sharp, pointed leaves and stems that are 0.7 to 2.4 inches (2 to 6cm) long.

Plants that live in still water often are not rooted to the bottom. Instead, they float on the surface of the water. One such plant is the water soldier, which gets its name from its pointed, bladelike leaves that

Water moss is a dark green aquatic plant that attaches itself to rocks.

look like swords. Each leaf is about 1 inch (2.5cm) wide, and the plant can reach up to 18 inches (45.7cm) in diameter. This plant flowers in the summer. Then it sinks to the bottom and stays there until spring, when it rises to the surface again.

The water soldier sinks to the bottom after flowering and resurfaces months later.

There are two basic types of plants in the ocean: those with roots attached to the seafloor and those that float. Seaweed, the ocean plant that most people are familiar with, is an example of the first type. Rootlike structures anchor it to rocks on the bottom of the ocean. An example of a floating sea plant is phytoplankton. These tiny, one-celled plants drift near the surface of the ocean, where sunlight penetrates the water. They use energy from the sun to change water and carbon dioxide into sugar and oxygen through photosynthesis. Some scientists believe that phytoplankton provides almost half of Earth's oxygen, because it is so plentiful in the ocean. Phytoplankton is also a primary food source for many ocean animals.

Life in the Water

Animals that live in water instead of on land have unique adaptations for aquatic life. All animals need oxygen to survive. Aquatic animals must get their oxygen by taking it in through the water or by surfacing and breathing oxygen in the air. They must also be able to move through the water. Some animals swim, others float, and still others rest on the bottom of their watery environment.

The blue tang's swim bladder keeps it afloat.

Fish, found in large numbers in the aquatic biome, have gills, rather than lungs, to get oxygen from the water. Gills are organs that resemble slits on the side of a fish's body. They allow oxygen and carbon dioxide to pass between the animal and the water surrounding it. Fish also have internal organs called swim bladders that help keep them afloat. Fish adjust the amount of air in their swim bladders so they can swim close to the surface or deeper in the water.

Like all fish, the tiger shark takes in oxygen from the water through its gills.

Aquatic animals also have other adaptations that allow them to thrive in their unique freshwater or marine environment. Fish that live in rivers and streams often have to deal with fast-moving currents. Some fish, such as trout, are able to swim against the current because they are shaped like a torpedo. This shape allows them to cut through the water and reduce the force of the water pushing against them. Other fish hug the river bottoms, where the water moves more slowly, because they cannot swim as well in the fast currents. The channel catfish of North America does this.

Like fish, many types of birds are well suited for life in lakes and ponds. One example of an aquatic bird is the northern pintail duck of North

Aquatic birds such as pintail ducks spend much of their time on the water.

Even though they live in the sea, dolphins are mammals, not fish.

America and Eurasia. The bird gets its name from its long, needle-like tail feathers. The pintail has a wide, round body that allows it to float on the water. It also has webbed feet for swimming. It hunts for insects and worms by immersing its head and upper body into the water while its legs kick in the air.

Ocean animals have challenges that freshwater animals do not have. One of these challenges is coping with a salty environment. Warm-blooded aquatic animals, such as birds and mammals, must have a source of freshwater, and they must be able

The albatross, the world's largest flying seabird, has glands on its beak that rid its body of excess salt.

to rid their bodies of excess salt. Dolphins get most of the freshwater they need from the flesh of the fish they eat. The albatross has special glands that rid its body of excess salt. These glands carry salt to the end of its beak, and the salty solution drips off.

Each of the five main biomes of Earth is unique. The animals and plants of each biome all contribute in their own way to the health of our planet.

Glossary

adaptations: Changes that occur over time in response to a certain environment.

camouflaged: Having coloring or other features that let an animal or plant blend in with its surroundings.

climate: The normal weather pattern for a region over a long period of time.

conifers: Needle-leaved trees that have seeds in their cones.

deciduous: Describes a plant that loses its leaves with the seasons.

droughts: Long periods without rain.

evaporation: To change from a liquid into a vapor or gas.

grazing: Feeding on growing plants.

marsupials: Animals that have a pouch on their abdomens for carrying their young.

migrate: To make a seasonal movement from one location to another.

photosynthesis: A process in which plants make their own food using sunlight.

precipitation: Hail, rain, sleet, or snow.

predators: Animals that hunt other animals for food.

prey: An animal that is eaten by another animal.

temperate: Describes a moderate climate that does not have extreme hot or cold temperatures.

tropical: Describes a hot, wet climate.

Books

Matt Doeden, *Grasslands*. Austin, TX: Raintree Steck-Vaughn, 2001. This book explores the climate, plants, and animals that make up the grasslands.

Philip Johansson, *The Frozen Tundra*. Berkeley Heights, NJ: Enslow, 2004. This book explores the special group of plants and animals that live in the tundra.

Angela Royston, *Extreme Survival Deserts*. Chicago: Raintree, 2004. This book explores how plants, animals, and people survive in the harsh desert environment.

Paul Stein, *Biomes of the Future*. New York: Rosen, 2001. A fascinating book that looks at the impact of changing weather patterns on the future of biomes.

Web Sites

Enchanted Learning (www.enchantedlearning. com). This site covers many educational subjects including biomes, oceans, and rain forests. There is a handy chart of the temperature, soil, plants, and animals of each biome.

Rainforest Heroes (www.rainforestheroes.com/ kidscorner/rainforests). This kid-friendly Web site contains a rain forest slide show. There is also an interactive map that shows the location of tropical, temperate, and boreal forests.

World Biomes (www.worldbiomes.com). This site provides detailed information about the five major biomes of the world. Colorful maps give an overview of the location of each biome. The site also has a useful list of frequently asked questions.

Index

Picture Credits

Cover photo: Taxi/Getty Images
© Bill Ross/CORBIS, 36
© Blickwindel/Alamy, 35
Corel Corp., 37
© George H.H. Huey/CORBIS, 18
Gregory G. Dimijian/Photo Researchers, Inc., 13
© Hal Beral/CORBIS, 38
© Jack Novak/CORBIS, 8
© James Randklev/CORBIS, 24–25
Joel Sartore/Getty Images, 32
© Joe McDonald/CORBIS, 30, 34
© Martin Harvey/CORBIS, 21
Maury Aasang, 6, 12, 20, 28
© Michael DeYoung/CORBIS, 7
National Geographic/Getty Images, 5
© Pat O'Hara/CORBIS, 27
© Paul A. Souders/CORBIS, 11
PhotoDisc, 15, 16, 31, 39, 40
R. Van Nostrand/Photo Researchers, Inc., 22
Stephen P. Parker/Photo Researchers, Inc., 27 (inset)
© Westend61/Alamy, 29
William Manning/CORBIS, 18 (inset)

Renee Kirchner has been writing stories, poems, and puzzles for children for four years. This is her first book for KidHaven Press. She holds a B.A. in marketing from Texas Tech University, and she works as a learning center manager at Rosemeade Elementary School. She lives with her husband and two children in Carrollton, Texas.